CARING FOR TAMARIN AS PET

SELECTING AND MAINTAINING TAMARINS AS PETS AND A COMPREHENSIVE GUIDE TO THEIR HABITAT, DIET, REPRODUCTION, AND MANY MORE INCLUDED

DR HUNTER DAVIS

Table of Contents

Introduction

Known for their colorful antics, distinct social structures, and endearing charm, tamarinds are a unique species that have become more and more popular as exotic pets in homes. However, despite their allure, prospective pet owners should be aware of the responsibilities and considerations involved in caring for these unique creatures. Tamarins are small monkeys that belong to the New World monkey family.

This in-depth guide will explore the world of tamarin pets and offer insightful information about their needs, behavior, and care. Whether you're new to primates or an experienced exotic pet enthusiast, it will hopefully provide you with the knowledge and comprehension required to give these amazing animals the best care possible.

Every facet of tamarin care will be thoroughly covered, from choosing the ideal species to setting up appropriate housing, providing appropriate nutrition, attending to medical needs, and developing deep bonds. We'll also go over important subjects like enrichment, training, breeding considerations, and legal responsibilities, so you'll be ready to start a rewarding journey as a tamarin pet owner.

Join us as we embark on this adventure, unraveling the mysteries of tamarin care and celebrating the joy that comes from sharing our lives with these extraordinary beings. By immersing ourselves in the fascinating realm of tamarins, we not only enhance our understanding of these captivating creatures but also enrich our lives through the unique companionship they offer.

Chapter 1

How to Choose the Correct Tamarin Species

The journey to owning a tamarin begins with choosing the right species. There are over 40 different species of tamarins that live in the tropical forests of Central and South America, each with their own distinct traits and needs, so before making a decision, you should carefully consider things like temperament, size, social structure, and suitability for your lifestyle. In this extensive guide, we'll go through the diverse world of tamarin species, offering in-depth information about their behavior, care requirements, and suitability as pets. By knowing the subtle differences between each species, you'll be better prepared to make an informed decision and start a rewarding journey with the ideal primate companion.

I. Tamarin Species Overview

First, let's review the taxonomy, distribution, and general characteristics of tamarin species. Tamarins are members of the Callitrichidae family, which also includes marmosets, and are further divided into several genera, including Saguinus and Leontopithecus. Although tamarins have many characteristics in common, like being small and having arboreal habits and omnivorous diets, each species has special adaptations that have been shaped by its particular environment.

II. Frequently Found Tamarin Species in Pet Trade

Callithrix jacchus, the common marmoset

Overview: Native to Brazil's northeastern forests, the common marmoset, also called the white-tufted marmoset, is one of the most common tamarin species kept as pets. These small primates are distinguished by their unique facial features and white tufts of hair on their ears.

Behavior and Temperament: Known for their lively and inquisitive nature, common marmosets live in family groups consisting of a breeding pair and their offspring. They are also highly social animals that frequently engage in playful behaviors and vocalizations.

Care Requirements: Fruits, insects, and small vertebrates are the main foods for common marmosets, who also benefit from routine veterinary check-ups to stay healthy. They need large enclosures with lots of climbing structures and enrichment opportunities.

Tamarin Cotton-Top (Saguinus oedipus)

Overview: Native to Colombia's tropical forests, the cotton-top tamarin is named for the unique white hair crest on its head. Known for its eye-catching appearance and energetic personality, this species has become more and more popular as a pet in recent years.

Behavior and Temperament: Cotton-top tamarins are vocal communicators, using chirps, trills, and alarm calls to convey messages to other members of their family group. They are also highly social animals that display complex social behaviors within their family groups.

Care Requirements: A varied diet of fruits, vegetables, insects, and commercial primate pellets is essential for the health and well-being of cotton-top tamarins, which need to be kept in large, multi-level enclosures with plenty of room for climbing and exploring.

III. Considerations for Selecting a Tamarin Species

Size and Space Requirements: Take into account the size of the tamarin species and make sure you have enough room to meet their housing requirements. Larger species might need enclosures that are larger and have more vertical space for climbing and exploring.

Temperament and Social Structure: To assess which tamarin species are suitable as pets, consider their temperament and social dynamics. Common marmosets, for example, are highly social and thrive in group environments, while other species may be more solitary or territorial.

Dietary Needs and Feeding Habits: To make sure you can give your tamarin a healthy, balanced diet, find out what foods they prefer to eat. Some species may have particular dietary needs, like a predilection for particular fruits or insects.

Activity Level and Enrichment Needs: Take into account the tamarin species' needs for mental and physical stimulation by providing opportunities for mental and physical stimulation through enrichment activities like puzzle feeders, climbing structures, and foraging. These activities can also help prevent boredom and encourage natural behaviors.

Compatibility with Other Pets: If you have other animals in your home, think about how well the tamarin species gets along with them. Some tamarin species get along well with other animals, while others might need to be introduced and supervised carefully.

IV. Making a Well-Informed Choice

Consider contacting reliable breeders or rescue groups that specialize in tamarin rehabilitation and rehoming. Before choosing a tamarin species as a pet, take the time to thoroughly research and educate yourself about the species' unique needs and requirements. Consult reputable sources such as primate care guides, experienced tamarin owners, and veterinary professionals specializing in exotic animal care.

Tamarin ownership is a long-term commitment, and providing appropriate care and enrichment is essential for the health and well-being of these intelligent and charismatic primates. You can make an informed decision and choose the right tamarin species to suit your preferences and circumstances by carefully considering factors like temperament, size, social structure, dietary needs, and compatibility with your lifestyle.

Whether you're drawn to the energetic nature of common marmosets or captivated by the striking appearance of cotton-top tamarins, each species offers its own rewards and challenges. With careful research, preparation, and dedication, you can embark on a fulfilling journey as a tamarin owner, forging a deep and meaningful bond with your primate companion for years to come. Choosing the right tamarin species is an important step in the journey to become a tamarin owner. This will help you make an informed decision and choose the ideal primate companion to enrich your life.

Chapter 2

Enclosure and Housing Requirements

Tamarins are arboreal primates with active lifestyles, so they need large, stimulating environments that resemble their natural habitats. In this thorough guide, we'll go over the important factors and specifications for housing and enclosures, so tamarin owners can create a safe, stimulating, and comfortable living space for their primate companions. Providing appropriate housing and enclosure is essential for the health, safety, and well-being of tamarin pets.

I. Recognizing the Habitat and Behavior of Tamarins

Tamarins live in dense tropical forests in Central and South America, where they spend most of their time in the canopy foraging for food, interacting with other members of their group, and seeking shelter from predators. Because they are highly arboreal animals, tamarins are adapted to climb, leap, and navigate complex tree structures, so having plenty of vertical space and opportunities for movement is crucial when designing an enclosure for a tamarin pet.

II. Size and Configuration of the Enclosure

The size of the enclosure will depend on the species and number of tamarins housed there; as a general rule, a single tamarin should have a minimum enclosure size of at least 4 feet tall by 4 feet wide by 6 feet long, with additional space required for each additional tamarin. Size Requirements: Tamarin enclosures should provide ample space for natural behaviors such as climbing, jumping, and exploring.

Vertical Space: Since tamarins are skilled climbers, enclosures with multiple levels, platforms, branches, and ropes will allow tamarins to freely explore their surroundings and move around. Adding different heights and textures will also encourage tamarins to climb, jump, and exercise, which will promote both physical and mental stimulation.

Enclosure Configuration: To create retreat areas where tamarins can rest, relax, and engage in natural behaviors, consider incorporating hiding spots, nesting boxes, and hammocks. Additionally, make sure the enclosure is made of sturdy materials and is escape-proof to prevent injury or accidental escape. Tamarin enclosures should be designed to maximize usable space while providing opportunities for privacy, enrichment, and social interaction.

III. Flooring and Substratum

Substrate Selection: Select a substrate that is safe, cozy, and low maintenance. Naturalistic materials that mimic the look and feel of the forest floor, like shredded paper, coconut fiber, or cypress mulch, work well for tamarin enclosures. Avoid materials that are dusty, abrasive, or harmful to tamarins, like sand, gravel, or cedar shavings.

Flooring Considerations: To minimize harm and promote healthy feet, tambin enclosures should have solid flooring. Solid flooring materials like hardwood, laminate, or non-toxic sealed concrete, enhanced with soft bedding or substrate for added comfort, are preferable to wire mesh flooring, which can lead to foot injuries and discomfort.

IV. Climbing Frameworks and Improving

Natural Branches and Perches: To give tamarins opportunities for climbing, balancing, and perching, incorporate natural branches, logs, and perches into the enclosure. Choose branches with different thicknesses and textures to replicate the variety of tree branches found in the tamarins' natural habitat. Make sure that branches are securely fastened to the enclosure to avoid collapse or injury.

Rope Swings and Ladders: To provide a sense of complexity and variation to a tamarin's surroundings, incorporate rope swings, ladders, and bridges. These structures not only promote natural behaviors like swinging, climbing, and exploring, but they also offer opportunities for enrichment and exercise. To ensure longevity and safety, use durable materials like sisal rope.

Enrichment Accessories: Add some fun and excitement to the tamarin's environment by adding interactive devices, puzzle feeders, and foraging toys. These enrichment tools promote problem-solving abilities, prevent boredom, and stop stereotypical behaviors. Make sure to rotate the enrichment items frequently to keep the tamarin's environment fresh and interesting.

V. Stimuli and Environmental Enrichment

Natural Light and Ventilation: Tamarin enclosures should be placed in areas with good lighting and direct sunlight, as this supports the production of vitamin D and healthy circadian rhythms. Adequate ventilation is also important to maintain the best possible air quality and avoid the accumulation of smells and humidity.

Visual and Auditory Stimuli: Give tamarins visual and auditory stimuli that replicate the sights and sounds of their natural habitat. You can enhance the tamarin's auditory experience by playing recorded sounds of birds, insects, and other forest noises. You can also decorate the enclosure with live or artificial plants, naturalistic decorations, and mirrors to create a visually stimulating environment.

Socialization: Provide opportunities for grooming, play, and communication; spend time interacting with tamarins every day through positive reinforcement training, enrichment activities, and bonding sessions. Tamarins are highly social animals and thrive on social interaction with conspecifics and human caregivers.

VI. Upkeep and Sanitization

Regular Maintenance: To maintain the tamarin enclosure's health and hygiene, set up a routine that includes weekly thorough cleanings of the enclosure, daily removals of waste, food debris, and soiled bedding, and disinfection of surfaces using safe and efficient cleaners that are advised for use in animal habitats.

Safety Inspections: To ensure that the enclosure is safe and functional, perform routine safety inspections to find and fix any potential hazards or structural problems. Look for loose or damaged parts, sharp edges, gaps, or openings that could endanger the well-being of tamarinds. Replace or repair any worn-out or damaged materials right away.

The health, safety, and well-being of tamarin pets depend on the provision of suitable housing and enclosure. Owners can create a safe, stimulating, and comfortable living space for their primate companions by learning about tamarin habitat and behavior, choosing enclosure size and configuration, and adding climbing structures, enrichment, and environmental stimuli. With regular upkeep and care, tamarin enclosures can offer tamarins a fulfilling and enriching environment that supports their physical, mental, and emotional needs, fostering a strong and enduring bond between tamarin and owner.

Chapter 3

Guidelines for Nutrition and Feeding

As omnivorous primates with a variety of dietary preferences, tamarins need a balanced and varied diet that meets their nutritional needs and supports their unique physiology. In this extensive guide, we'll explore the key principles and considerations for feeding and nutrition, giving tamarin owners the knowledge and resources necessary to ensure optimal health and well-being for their primate companions. Feeding and nutrition play a vital role in the health, well-being, and longevity of tamarin pets.

I. Recognizing the Dietary Needs for Tamarins

Prior to discussing specific feeding guidelines, it is important to comprehend the dietary needs of tamarin species. Tamarins eat a variety of foods in the wild, including fruits, insects, gums, nectar, and small vertebrates, depending on the species, habitat, and season. They are opportunistic feeders, meaning they have evolved to take advantage of a wide range of food sources and have modified their feeding behaviors to fit their surroundings.

II. Elements of a Well-Rounded Diet

Fruits and Vegetables: When it comes to vitamins, minerals, and fiber, fresh fruits and vegetables should be the cornerstone of a tamarin's diet. Provide a range of fruits, including bananas, apples, grapes, oranges, mangoes, and berries, along with leafy greens, carrots, bell peppers, and squash. The goal is to offer a diverse selection of fruits and vegetables to ensure nutritional variety and prevent dietary deficiencies.

Protein Sources: Lean meats (e.g., chicken, turkey), fish, cooked legumes (e.g., lentils, chickpeas, black beans), insects (e.g., crickets, mealworms, and waxworms) can all be provided as occasional treats or enrichment items. Tamarins need high-protein diets to support muscle growth, repair, and general health.

Commercial Primate Pellets: If you are looking for a convenient and nutritionally balanced staple for your tamarins' diet, consider commercial primate pellets that are specifically formulated for them. Look for high-quality pellets that contain a balanced blend of vitamins, minerals, protein, and fiber. You can offer pellets as a supplementary food source in addition to fresh fruits, vegetables, and protein-rich foods.

Supplements and Treats: To support bone health and prevent deficiencies, sparingly offer treats like nuts, seeds, dried fruits, and yogurt drops as occasional rewards or treats during training sessions. Additionally, think about supplementing tamarin diets with calcium and vitamin D3 supplements. Speak with a veterinarian who specializes in exotic animal nutrition to determine appropriate supplementation.

III. Mealtime Routine and Quantities

Frequency: Although free-feeding or leaving food out for long periods of time can encourage overeating and obesity, tamarinds are usually fed multiple small meals throughout the day to mimic their natural feeding behavior. Provide fresh food and water in the morning and evening, with additional snacks or treats provided as enrichment throughout the day.

Portion Sizes: Pay close attention to portion sizes to avoid overfeeding or underfeeding. Provide food in amounts that are appropriate for the tamarin's size, age, activity level, and dietary needs. You can also make necessary adjustments based on the tamarin's personal preferences, metabolic rate, and body condition score.

Feeding Enrichment: Food items can be hidden within enrichment devices or scattered throughout the enclosure to encourage tamarins to search, explore, and participate in problem-solving activities. Feeding enrichment activities include puzzle feeders, foraging toys, and food puzzles.

IV. Water and Hydration Needs

Access to Fresh Water: Make sure tamarins always have access to clean, fresh water. Water can be offered in shallow bowls or in bottles that are attached to the enclosure to make drinking easier. Keep an eye on water consumption and replenish water sources as needed to keep tamarins hydrated.

Hydration Monitoring: Keep an eye on your temperate pet's fluid intake and behavior. Symptoms of dehydration include lethargy, sunken eyes, dry skin, and decreased urine production. If you suspect dehydration, give your pet more fluids and seek veterinary advice for a thorough examination and treatment.

V. Particular Occupations and Dietary Guidelines

Dietary Restrictions: Depending on their natural habitat, physiology, or health status, some tamarin species may have particular dietary requirements or restrictions. For instance, species that primarily rely on gums or nectar in the wild may need special diets or supplements to replicate these food sources in captivity. To create a customized diet plan for tamarins with special dietary needs, consult a veterinarian or primate nutritionist.

Allergies and Sensitivities: Just like people, tamarons may become allergic to certain foods or ingredients. It is important to keep a close eye on your tamarind's behavior and digestive system when introducing new foods or changing their diet. If your tamarind exhibits any signs of an allergic reaction or upset stomach, cut out the offending food item from their diet and seek advice from a veterinarian.

VI. Tracking and Modifying the Diet

Frequent Monitoring: Keep detailed records of food consumption, weight fluctuations, and any changes in appetite or feeding behavior. Regularly monitor the body condition, behavior, and general health of tamarinds to evaluate the efficacy of their diet and feeding regimen.

Dietary Changes: Depending on the tamarin's unique needs, preferences, and health, make dietary changes as necessary. For advice on maximizing nutrient intake, correcting any nutritional imbalances or deficiencies, speak with a veterinarian or primate nutritionist.

Tamarin owners can support optimal physical health, cognitive function, and emotional well-being for their primate companions by providing a balanced and varied diet that meets their nutritional needs. Tamarin owners can also ensure that their pets thrive on a diet that nourishes both body and mind by paying close attention to dietary requirements, feeding schedules, portion sizes, and dietary enrichment. Feeding and nutrition are critical aspects of tamarin care that have a significant impact on the health, well-being, and longevity of these amazing primates.

Chapter 4

Veterinary Care and Tamarin Health

Veterinary care and tamarin health are essential components of responsible tamarin ownership. These fascinating primates need careful and proactive healthcare to maintain optimal well-being throughout their lives because of their intricate social structures and distinctive physiological traits. We'll go over the main ideas and factors pertaining to tamarin health and veterinary care in this extensive guide, giving tamarin owners the information and tools they need to make sure their primates live long and healthy lives.

I. Comprehending the Physiology and Behavior of Tamarins

Understanding the physiology and behavior of tamarins is crucial before diving into specific health and veterinary care guidelines. Tamarins are arboreal primates that are indigenous to tropical forests in Central and South America. Because of these adaptations, they have specific needs that affect their health and upkeep. Tamarins display a variety of behaviors and traits that influence how they interact with their surroundings and caretakers, from their quick climbing skills to their complex social dynamics.

II. Preventive Health Actions

Frequent Vet Check-ups: Arrange for tamarins to undergo regular veterinary examinations in order to keep an eye on their general health, spot early warning indicators of disease, and take proactive measures to address any health issues. A thorough physical examination that evaluates oral health, musculoskeletal function, and body condition can help detect possible health problems before they become more serious.

Vaccinations and Preventive Care: To ascertain the proper vaccination schedule and preventive care protocols for tamarins, speak with a veterinarian who specializes in exotic animal medicine. Although there aren't any vaccinations made especially for tamarinds, some vets might advise vaccinating against common infectious diseases or parasites depending on the tamarind's exposure and risk factors.

Implement a parasite control program to stop infestations of ticks, mites, and gastrointestinal worms, among other external and internal parasites. As directed by a veterinarian, administer antiparasitic drugs and conduct routine fecal examinations to check for parasite eggs or larvae.

Dental Care: Encourage natural chewing behavior in tamarins by giving them toys and enrichment materials that are safe for their teeth. Regularly check the health of your pet's teeth and seek veterinary advice if you notice any symptoms of dental disease, such as tartar accumulation, discolored teeth, or trouble eating.

Environmental Hygiene: Keep the tamarins' enclosure, food and water dishes, and enrichment materials clean and hygienic by cleaning and disinfecting them on a regular basis. To reduce the risk of infectious diseases and avoid bacterial contamination, throw away food debris, soiled bedding, and excrement as soon as possible.

III. Typical Health Problems with Tamarins

Dental Illness: Tamarins are vulnerable to dental issues like malocclusion, periodontal disease, and tooth decay, which can cause discomfort, infection, and trouble eating. Keep a close eye on your pet's dental health and contact a veterinarian if you notice any warning signs of dental disease, such as drooling, reluctance to eat, or changes in chewing habits.

Gastrointestinal Disorders: Infectious agents, stress, and poor diet choices can cause tamarinds to suffer from gastrointestinal disorders like diarrhea, constipation, or bloating. If gastrointestinal abnormalities continue or get worse, keep an eye on the quantity, consistency, and frequency of tamarind feces and seek advice from a veterinarian.

Tamarins are prone to respiratory infections brought on by bacteria, viruses, or fungi. These infections can cause symptoms like sneezing, coughing, nasal discharge, and trouble breathing. Tamarins should have a clean, well-ventilated environment, and if respiratory symptoms are noticed, they should be taken to the vet right away.

Parasitic Infestations: Tamarins are susceptible to both external and internal parasite infestations, including ticks and mites, as well as roundworms, tapeworms, and coccidia. Administer antiparasitic treatments as directed by a veterinarian and keep an eye out for symptoms of parasitic infestation, such as poor appetite, weight loss, itching, or skin lesions, in tamarin health and behavior.

IV. Veterinary Medicine and Care

Veterinary Exam: Select a veterinarian with experience and training in treating exotic animals, especially primates, when seeking veterinary care for tamarins. To determine the tamarin's general health, identify any underlying medical issues, and create a suitable treatment plan, schedule a thorough veterinary examination.

Diagnostic Testing: To further assess the tamarind's health and find underlying medical conditions, diagnostic tests like blood work, fecal analysis, radiography, or ultrasound may be suggested based on their symptoms and clinical presentation.

Treatment Options: Depending on the type and severity of the condition, treatment options for tamarin health issues may involve medication, surgery, supportive care, or dietary changes. Create a treatment plan in close consultation with your veterinarian that is specific to the needs and circumstances of your tamarin.

Post-treatment Care: Pay close attention to your veterinarian's instructions on medication administration, follow-up appointments, and post-treatment care. Keep a close eye on the tamarin's development and notify your veterinarian right away of any changes in behavior, appetite, or symptoms.

V. First Aid and Emergency Preparedness

Create an emergency response plan that outlines contacts for local wildlife authorities, veterinary clinics, and poison control centers in case of tamarin health emergencies. Learn the typical symptoms of illness or distress in tamarins so you can recognize when to seek emergency veterinary care.

First Aid Supplies: Always have a fully supplied first aid kit on hand with items like gloves, sterile gauze pads, bandages, tweezers, and antiseptic solution. While you wait for veterinary care, be ready to provide basic first aid in the event of wounds, injuries, or emergencies.

Emergency Transport: When taking tamarins to veterinarian appointments or emergency care facilities, have a suitable and safe transport carrier or enclosure on hand. To avoid harm during transit, make sure the carrier is cushioned, escape-proof, and has adequate ventilation.

VI. Environmental and Behavioral Factors

Reduce the amount of stress in the tamarin's surroundings and offer it chances for socialization, mental stimulation, and rest. To support emotional well-being, minimize abrupt changes or disruptions to their routine and offer consistent, enriching experiences.

Environmental Enrichment: Provide foraging, puzzle feeders, climbing frames, and socializing opportunities to improve the tamarin's surroundings. Tamarins can benefit from mental and physical exercise, as well as sensory experiences and cognitive challenges.

Tamarins are gregarious creatures that benefit greatly from social contact with both human caretakers and other conspecifics. This leads to socialization and bonding. Through interactive play, grooming sessions, and positive reinforcement training, you can enhance the human-animal bond and foster trust and companionship by spending quality time with tamarins.

To ensure the health and longevity of these amazing primates, tamarin ownership requires proper veterinary care and tamarin health. Tamarin owners can protect the health and well-being of their primates by putting preventive health measures into place, keeping an eye out for common health problems, getting quick veterinary care when necessary, and creating a nurturing and stimulating environment. Tamarins can flourish in captivity and provide their human caregivers with years of happiness, companionship, and enrichment if they receive proactive healthcare and attentive management.

Chapter 5

Improvement and Mental Excitation

Essential components of tamarin care include enrichment and mental stimulation, which enhance the general health, happiness, and well-being of these socially adept and intelligent primates. Tamarins thrive in environments that allow for exploration, problem-solving, and social interaction because of their complex cognitive abilities and curious nature. We'll examine the ideas and methods for enhancing tamarin pets' lives in this extensive guide, making sure they have a happy, engaging environment that encourages their innate behaviors and cognitive growth.

I. Recognizing the Natural History and Behavior of Tamarins

Prior to diving into particular enrichment methods, it's critical to comprehend tamarin behavior and natural history. Tamarins are arboreal primates that are indigenous to the tropical forests of Central and South America. They have evolved extensively to live in the canopy, where they carry out foraging, grooming, socializing, and defending their territory. Within their family groups, tamarinds display intricate social structures. They depend on social bonds, cooperation, and communication to navigate their surroundings and interact with other tamarinds.

II. Enrichment Principles

Variety: To keep tamarins interested and stimulated, provide a range of enrichment experiences, materials, and activities. To keep enrichment items fresh and avoid habituation, rotate them frequently to keep tamarins interested and challenged.

Give tamarins the ability to make decisions and take charge of their surroundings. Provide a variety of enrichment materials, including toys, puzzles, and climbing frames, and let tamarins choose activities according to their own interests and preferences.

Complexity: Provide mentally and physically demanding enrichment activities that motivate tamarins to solve problems, explore, and manipulate objects. Incorporate elements of challenge, complexity, and unpredictability to encourage behavioral flexibility and cognitive development.

Safety: Make sure that every activity and item for enrichment is suitable for the age, temperament, and species of tamarins. Enrichment sessions should involve careful observation of tamarin behavior and prompt removal of any potential hazards or safety concerns.

III. Techniques for Enriching the Environment

Opportunities for Foraging: Encourage natural foraging habits by concealing food in puzzle feeders, enrichment devices, or foraging toys. Encourage tamarins to scavenge, investigate, and alter their surroundings in order to retrieve food rewards, thereby fostering cognitive and motor stimulation.

Climbing Structures: Build platforms, ropes, branches, and climbing structures into the enclosure to give tamarins the chance to swing, climb, and jump. Construct multi-level settings with different textures and heights to evoke the intricacy of the forest canopy and promote organic movement.

Treat balls, puzzle feeders, and interactive toys that need tamarins to manipulate objects, solve puzzles, or extract food rewards are all good options. Engage the tamarin's dexterity and problem-solving abilities while offering mental stimulation and enrichment.

Novel Materials and Objects: To pique a tamarin's interest and encourage exploration, surround them with new materials, textures, scents, and objects. Give tamarins objects to explore, play with, and investigate, such as cardboard boxes, paper bags, PVC tubes, and natural foliage.

Opportunities for Socialization: Assist tamarins in developing strong bonds and fostering social interaction by placing them in groups or pairs that get along well as by giving them opportunities for play, grooming, and communication. Plan enrichment activities that promote collaboration and fortify social ties among group members.

IV. Enhancement of Senses

Visual Stimulation: Incorporate mirrors, bright objects, and visual barriers into the tamarin's surroundings to stimulate its sense of sight. By changing the colors, forms, and patterns of enrichment items, you can add visual complexity and interest while enticing tamarins to explore and learn about their surroundings.

Auditory Stimulation: Add natural sounds, like bird calls, insect noises, and forest sounds, to the tamarin's auditory environment. In order to create a sensory-rich environment that encourages tamarin auditory perception and engagement, play recorded audio tracks or live streams of natural sounds.

Olfactory Stimulation: Introduce aromas and scents from plants, such as flowers, fruits, and herbs, to improve the tamarin's sense of smell. Provide opportunities for scent-marking, scent trails, and scented enrichment items to stimulate tamarin's sense of smell and encourage curiosity.

V. Enhancement of Cognitive Ability

Training and Enrichment Sessions: Train tamarins through positive reinforcement to promote learning, cognitive engagement, and the development of new skills. Tamarins can be trained to carry out basic tasks like stationing, target training, and object retrieval. Successful completion of these tasks will be rewarded with praise or treats.

Tasks for Solving Problems: Give tamarins cognitive exercises that call for forethought, planning, and memory. Provide tamarins with puzzle feeders, maze toys, or food-dispensing devices to help them solve puzzles and plan ahead in order to get food rewards.

Environmental Modifications: Tamarins' cognitive capacities and adaptability can be stimulated by making periodic changes or alterations to their surroundings. Arrange furniture in a different way, replace enrichment items, or add new materials and objects to encourage tamarins to investigate, explore, and adjust to changes in their environment.

VI. Observation and Assessment

Behavioral Observation: Pay close attention to tamarin behavior during enrichment sessions to gauge their degree of interaction, engagement, and interest with the items being enhanced. Keep an eye on how tamarinds react to various forms of enrichment, and modify activities in response to their input and preferences.

Behavioral Assessments: To determine the success of enrichment programs and pinpoint areas for development, conduct regular behavioral assessments, also known as enrichment evaluations. To record tamarin behavior and monitor alterations over time, use ethograms or standardized behavioral scoring systems.

Feedback and Adaptation: To obtain opinions and insights regarding the appropriateness and efficacy of enrichment, ask veterinary professionals, tamarin caregivers, and enrichment specialists for their thoughts. Programs for enrichment should be modified in response to comments, observations, and continuing evaluations of tamarin behavioral responses.

Essential elements of tamarin care include mental stimulation and enrichment, which support natural behaviors, cognitive growth, and psychological health. Tamarin owners can improve their monkey companions' quality of life and happiness by creating an environment that is both stimulating and enriching, incorporating a range of sensory, social, cognitive, and environmental stimuli. A strong and meaningful bond between tamarins and their human caregivers can be fostered by tamarin caregivers through the careful planning, inventiveness, and observation of enriching experiences that engage, challenge, and inspire tamarins to thrive in captivity.

Chapter 6

Bonding and Socialization with Your Tamarin

In order to create deep and meaningful relationships between tamarins and their human caregivers, socialization and bonding are crucial components of tamarin care. Tamarins are highly gregarious and intelligent primates that enjoy interacting socially and communicating with humans as well as other members of their own species. We'll go over the fundamentals and techniques of socializing and bonding with tamarin pets in this extensive guide, building a solid and dependable relationship built on affection, respect, and understanding.

I. Comprehending the Social Behavior of Tamarins

Prior to diving into particular socialization methods, it's critical to comprehend tamarin social dynamics and behavior. A breeding pair and their young make up cohesive family groups in the wild, where tamarins engage in a variety of social activities like play, vocalizations, grooming, and territorial defense. Tamarins navigate their environment, create hierarchies, and uphold group cohesiveness through communication, cooperation, and social bonds.

II. Socialization Principles

Patience and Respect: When socializing with tamarins, exercise patience, show them respect, and be mindful of their personal boundaries and preferences. Tamarins should be given the freedom to initiate interactions at their own pace; do not overburden or force them with unwelcome attention or handling.

Positive Reinforcement: To reinforce desired behaviors and motivate tamarins to interact with others, use positive reinforcement techniques like treats, praise, and rewards. Provide incentives to tamarins who approach, engage with, or react favorably to humans, progressively fostering a sense of confidence and trust.

Routine and Consistency: Create a predictable and steady schedule for your interactions with tamarins, and include daily bonding activities in their daily care routine. Tamarins benefit from consistency in their surroundings because it lowers stress levels and encourages relaxation during socialization activities.

Observation and Communication: Tamarins can convey their mood, comfort level, and communication cues through their body language, vocalizations, and facial expressions. Pay great attention to these cues. Show empathy, understanding, and make the necessary behavioral and interactional adjustments in response to tamarin signals and cues.

III. Bonding Methods

Respectful Approach: To avoid frightening or startling tamarins, approach them quietly and gently. Use slow, non-threatening movements and body language. Respect their personal space and boundaries and allow tamarins to approach you voluntarily and initiate contact on their terms.

Hand-feeding: During feeding sessions, offer food rewards from your hand to tamarins to establish rapport and trust. Tamarins can be encouraged to approach you and accept food by offering them small, bite-sized treats like fruits, nuts, or mealworms. Gradually increase the amount of physical contact with them as you do this.

Grooming and Touch: Start mild grooming sessions with tamarinds to imitate their family groups' natural social behaviors, like allo-grooming. Tamarin fur can be gently stroked with your fingers or a soft grooming brush; pay particular attention to the head, shoulders, and back. Introduce light touch and physical contact gradually, taking into account the comfort levels and reactions of tamarinds.

Interactive Play: Take tamarins on interactive play sessions that promote movement, socialization, and inquiry. Engage tamarins' natural behaviors and spark their curiosity with toys, puzzles, and enrichment items. This will encourage them to interact with you in a playful and positive way.

IV. Developing Self-Belief and Trust

Respect Boundaries: Be mindful of the preferences and limits of tamarinds when it comes to handling, physical contact, and interaction. Let tamarins dictate the speed and degree of socialization; with time, positive reinforcement and experiences will gradually raise the degree of comfort and trust.

Avoid Punishment: During socialization, refrain from employing punishment or negative reinforcement methods as these can erode trust, exacerbate fear, and weaken the bond between tamarins and their caregivers. Rather, concentrate on rewarding desired conduct and creating favorable connections with interpersonal communication.

Regularly spending time with tamarins will strengthen your bond and familiarity with them. This is known as Consistent Presence. To improve the human-tamarin bond, schedule regular bonding sessions where you spend time engaging, playing, and chatting with tamarins.

Respect Individuality: Take note of and show consideration for the unique temperaments, inclinations, and personalities of tamarins; modify your approach and manner of interacting with them accordingly. While some tamarins may be more gregarious and extroverted, others may be more cautious or reserved, necessitating tolerance and understanding during socialization.

V. Interaction and Comprehension

Tamarin vocalizations and vocal cues can indicate a variety of needs, desires, and intentions, so pay attention to them. Acquire the ability to decipher and react appropriately to common tamarin vocalizations, including chirps, trills, alarm calls, and contact calls.

Body Language: Tamarins' mood, behavior, and degree of comfort can all be inferred from their postures and body language during socialization. Look for indicators of stress or discomfort, such as tense posture, flattened ears, or avoidance behavior, as well as indicators of relaxation, curiosity, and engagement, such as open mouth, bright eyes, and relaxed posture.

Exercises and activities aimed at fostering mutual understanding, cooperation, and bonding between you and tamarins are good ways to establish trust. Engage in positive and cooperative interactions with tamarins by practicing activities like cooperative feeding, target training, and clicker training.

Mutual Respect: Establish clear communication, empathy, and understanding as the foundation for a cooperative, mutually respectful relationship with tamarins. By treating tamarins as unique people with their own ideas, emotions, and preferences, you can cultivate a relationship based on respect and camaraderie.

VI. Establishing a Bonding Practice

Creating a Routine: Create a daily routine for bonding with tamarins by introducing interactions, structured activities, and enrichment opportunities into their daily care schedule. Plan your bonding activities for regular times throughout the day to give tamarins structure and predictability.

Spend quality time with tamarins, emphasizing the development of positive associations, trust, and connection via play, communication, and gentle interaction. Establish a peaceful, unhurried atmosphere free from interruptions and distractions for bonding activities.

Enrichment Activities: To encourage tamarin engagement, curiosity, and exploration, incorporate enrichment activities into bonding sessions. To foster playful and stimulating interactions with tamarins and to fortify your bond, use interactive games, puzzles, and toys.

Tamarins can learn about new places, sights, and smells by going on supervised outdoor excursions or outings. Give tamarins the chance to interact with nature and partake in supervised outdoor activities like climbing, foraging, and sunbathing.

Bonding and socializing with tamarins are fulfilling and enriching experiences that promote companionship, trust, and mutual understanding between tamarins and their human caregivers. Tamara owners can develop deep and meaningful relationships with their primate companions that are based on mutual trust, communication, and affection by approaching socialization with patience, respect, and empathy. Tamarin owners can enrich the lives of their tamarin companions as well as their own by forming a strong and enduring bond with their primates through consistent effort, positive reinforcement, and knowledge of tamarin behavior.

Chapter 7

Instruction and Behavioral Factors

In order to effectively communicate with tamarind pets, encourage desired behaviors, and deal with behavioral issues, training and behavioral considerations are essential. Tamarins can learn a wide range of behaviors through positive reinforcement training techniques because of their intelligence, curiosity, and social nature. We'll examine the fundamentals and methods of behavior control and training for tamarin pets in this extensive guide, equipping pet owners to create a positive and fulfilling bond with their primate friends.

I. Comprehending the Behavior of Tamarins

It's critical to comprehend tamarins' social dynamics and innate behavioral patterns before diving into training methods. Tamarins are intelligent, highly social primates that participate in a range of activities including grooming, socializing, foraging, and territorial defense. Tamarins use facial expressions, body language, and vocalizations as forms of communication. They use these cues to express emotions, convey information, and create social hierarchies within their family groups.

II. Fundamentals of Instruction

Positive Reinforcement: This type of training increases the probability that desired behaviors will occur in the future by providing treats, compliments, or other rewards. Tamarins find great motivation in rewards, so use mealworms, nuts, or tiny pieces of fruit to effectively reinforce desired behaviors.

Maintaining consistency is essential for effective tamarin training. To consistently communicate expectations and reinforce desired behaviors, use cues that are clear and consistent as well as reinforcement techniques. Tamarins may become confused and frustrated if training methods are inconsistent or send mixed signals.

Patience: Since teaching tamarins new behaviors takes time and repetition, training them requires both patience and persistence. When teaching tamarins new behaviors, be patient with them and offer them support and encouragement along the way.

Flexibility and adaptability are key components of a successful training program. Tamarins vary in temperament, individuality, and responsiveness, so be sure to modify techniques and strategies accordingly. To maximize success and engagement, customize training methods to each tamarin's unique needs, preferences, and learning styles.

III. Fundamental Exercise Methods

Teaching tamarins to touch or follow a target object—like a handheld stick or target stick—with their nose or hand is known as target training. Tamarins should be rewarded for approaching or touching the target object with their noses or hands when you first present it to them. By relocating the target object and rewarding progressively closer approximations of the desired behavior, you can gradually shape the behavior.

Teaching tamarins to stay in a specific location, or station, for a set amount of time is known as stationing. To begin, set up a target object (a mat or perch, for example) in the desired spot and offer rewards to tamarins who stay on or close to the station. Tamarins should spend more time at the station gradually to reinforce their calm, relaxed behavior.

Teaching tamarins to come when called or signaled is known as recall training. Start with a highly motivating reward combined with a unique recall cue, like a whistle or spoken command. As tamarins get better at recall exercises, gradually increase the distance and distractions in a controlled setting.

Techniques for desensitization and counterconditioning can be employed to assist tamarins in overcoming anxiety, fear, or aversion to particular stimuli or circumstances. Tamarins should be gradually exposed to the feared stimulus at a low intensity while being associated with positive experiences, like play or treats, to help them form positive associations and eventually become less fearful or anxious.

IV. Taking Care of Behavioral Issues

Aggression: Positive reinforcement training techniques that encourage composure and cooperative behavior while minimizing conflict can effectively address aggression in tamarins. Determine the factors that lead to aggressive behavior and put management techniques in place to reduce the likelihood of aggression, such as giving people enough space, fostering social interactions, and enriching their surroundings.

Fearfulness: Use counterconditioning and progressive desensitization techniques to help tamarins overcome their fearfulness by exposing them to feared stimuli in a positive and controlled way. Tamarins should be allowed to explore and become acclimated to new situations in a safe and encouraging environment. Treats and praise should be given for bold or self-assured behavior.

Destructive Behavior: Use positive reinforcement training, environmental enrichment, and diversionary strategies to manage and redirect destructive behaviors in tamarins. Reduce the opportunity for harmful behavior in the home by giving tamarins suitable outlets for their natural activities, such as climbing, foraging, and exploring.

Vocalizations: Use positive reinforcement training techniques to promote quiet, composed behavior in order to address excessive vocalizations or vocalizations linked to undesirable behaviors. By using cues like "quiet" or "calm" in conjunction with rewards, you can gradually decrease tamarin vocalizations by teaching them to stay quiet or composed in particular circumstances.

V. Instruction in Mental Stimulation and Enrichment

Enrichment Activities: Take advantage of training sessions to introduce tamarins to enrichment activities that encourage socialization, physical activity, and mental stimulation. To promote problem-solving, exploration, and engagement, include interactive toys, puzzle feeders, and environmental enrichment in training sessions.

Cognitive Challenges: To increase tamarin intelligence and cognitive capacities, incorporate problem-solving exercises and cognitive challenges into training sessions. Provide engaging and mentally stimulating interactive puzzles, maze toys, or training games for tamarins that need them to solve problems in order to win rewards.

Opportunities for Socialization: Make the most of training sessions to foster bonds and socialization between tamarins and their caregivers. Include activities such as cooperative training, group training, or interactive play that encourage tamarin and human social interaction, cooperation, and communication.

Emphasize skill development and lifelong learning for tamarins through continuous training and enrichment activities. Keep providing tamarins with novel experiences, activities, and behaviors to keep them mentally flexible, adaptive, and resilient throughout their lives.

VI. Observation and Assessment

Progress tracking: Using thorough training logs and behavioral observations, monitor the development, performance, and behavioral shifts of tamarinds over time. During training sessions, keep an eye on the tamarinds' responsiveness, engagement, and success rates. Based on their performance, modify tactics and strategies as necessary.

Feedback and Adaptation: Get opinions and insights regarding the suitability and efficacy of the training from behavior specialists, veterinary personnel, and caregivers of tamarinds. Programs for training should be modified in response to comments, observations, and continuing evaluations of tamarin behavioral responses and development.

Celebrate Your Success: Give praise, treats, or other incentives to acknowledge and celebrate your tamarin training accomplishments, no matter how small. To keep tamarins motivated and engaged, create a positive training environment, and fortify the bond between tamarins and their caregivers, consistently recognize and reinforce desirable behaviors.

In order to provide good communication, cooperation, and overall wellbeing for both tamarins and their caregivers, training and behavioral considerations are crucial parts of tamarin care. Tamarin owners can cultivate a happy and satisfying relationship with their primate companions by using positive reinforcement training methods, proactively addressing behavioral issues, and offering enriching training opportunities. Caregivers can improve the quality of life and bond between humans and tamarins by empowering tamarins to learn, grow, and thrive in captivity through patience, consistency, and understanding of tamarin behavior.

Chapter 8

Breeding and Reproduction of Tamarins

The intricate processes of tamarind reproduction and breeding are impacted by a number of variables, such as social dynamics, environmental circumstances, and individual traits. Tamarins are fascinating, gregarious primates with distinctive reproductive habits and life cycle patterns that are essential to the preservation and control of captive populations. We'll delve into the nuances of tamarin reproduction and breeding in this extensive guide, offering insights into their reproductive biology, behaviors, and care requirements for responsible ownership and successful breeding programs.

I. Tamarind Reproductive Biology

Understanding tamarin reproductive biology is crucial before discussing specific breeding considerations. Similar to other primates, tamarinds have an intricate reproductive system that is impacted by social interactions, hormonal cycles, and environmental cues. Typically, the menstrual cycle of female tamarins consists of ovulation and estrous periods, when the animals are open to mating. To attract mates and form breeding pairs, male tamarins engage in reproductive behaviors like scent-marking, vocalizations, and courtship displays.

II. Tamarin Life Cycle

Sexual Maturity: Tamarins typically reach sexual maturity between the ages of 18 and 24 months, though this can vary based on the species, genetics, and environment. Hormonal shifts, the emergence of secondary sexual traits, and behavioral cues indicating preparedness for reproduction are the hallmarks of sexual maturity.

Estrous Cycle: The receptivity and fertile phases of the female tamarin's estrous cycle normally occur at regular intervals. Different tamarin species and individuals have different estrous cycle lengths and timings, which range from roughly 14 to 21 days.

In order to attract female mates and form breeding pairs, male tamarins participate in courtship behaviors such as vocalizations, displays, and grooming during the breeding season. In order to prepare for copulation and mating, males and females may engage in scent-marking, chasing, and mutual grooming during courtship rituals.

Gestation and Birth: Depending on the species, female tamarins that successfully mate go through a gestation period that lasts between 140 and 170 days. Tamarins usually give birth to single babies, though sometimes they give birth to twins. The babies weigh between 15 and 35 grams when they are born. Certain tamarin species have year-round birthing, while others show seasonal breeding patterns related to climate and food availability.

Care and Development of the Infant: Tamarin babies are born altricial, with immature sensory and motor abilities, and they are dependent on their mothers for protection and care. Tamarin females give their young intensive maternal care, including nursing, grooming, carrying, and protecting them to make sure they are healthy and happy. Tamarin babies grow and develop quickly; during the first few months of life, they accomplish milestones like eye opening, independent walking, and weaning.

III. Breeding Factors to Consider When Owning a Tamarin

Pair Bonding: Create tamarin breeding pairs that are compatible with each other based on social compatibility, temperament, and genetics. Keep an eye on prospective breeding partners' social interactions and compatibility to ensure peaceful pair bonding and reduce hostility or conflict.

Enhancement of the Environment: Create a naturalistic setting with naturalistic elements, materials for nesting, and chances for socialization and exploration to give breeding tamarins a stimulating and enriching environment. Within the enclosure, construct nesting places or shelters to imitate natural nesting behaviors and give breeding pairs privacy and security.

Nutritional Support: Make sure that the diet of breeding tamarins is well-balanced and suited to their requirements for reproduction. This should include fresh produce, high-quality commercial primate pellets, and protein sources. See a veterinarian that specializes in exotic animal nutrition to create a diet that promotes healthy reproduction and produces the best possible offspring.

Monitoring Reproductive Cycles: Keep a close eye out for behavioral changes, vocalizations, and swelling in the genital area that may indicate estrus in female tamarins. Maintain thorough records of mating habits, reproductive cycles, and breeding results in order to monitor the success of breeding and spot any potential problems or difficulties.

Pregnancy Care: To protect the health and wellbeing of the mother and her developing offspring, give pregnant tamarins specialized care and support. Keep an eye out for symptoms of pregnancy-related problems in expectant mothers, such as weight loss, lethargy, or dystocia (difficult labor), and get veterinary help right away if something seems off.

IV. Strategies for Breeding Management

Controlled Breeding Programs: To preserve genetic diversity, reduce inbreeding, and promote long-term population sustainability, captive tamarin populations should be subject to controlled breeding programs. Collaborate on breeding initiatives with other recognized zoological establishments and breeding centers to share genetic resources and develop breeding guidelines grounded in genetic genealogy information.

Reproductive Health Monitoring: Perform routine screenings and assessments of reproductive health, such as hormone monitoring, ultrasounds, and fertility assessments, for tamarin breeding. Work together with veterinary specialists and experts in reproduction to identify and treat infertility or reproductive disorders that could affect the success of breeding.

Breeding Season Manipulation: To stimulate or synchronize breeding activity in captive tamarin populations, manipulate lighting cycles and environmental factors. To replicate seasonal cues and promote courtship, mating, and nesting—natural breeding behaviors—adjust photoperiods, temperature, and humidity levels.

Pregnancy status, birth outcomes, mating behavior, and breeding introductions should all be meticulously documented in your breeding management records. Track breeding information, pedigree details, and genetic lineage records for individual tamarins and breeding pairs using electronic databases or software programs.

V. Hand-rearing and Neonatal Care

Neonatal Care: To guarantee the health, survival, and well-being of newborn tamarin infants during the crucial neonatal period, provide them with specialized care and support. Newborns should be closely observed for indications of distress, hypothermia, or neglect by their mothers. If necessary, additional heat, hydration, and nutritional support should be given.

Maternal Bonding: Reduce disturbances and create a calm, safe space for mother-infant interactions in order to support maternal bonding and maternal care behaviors in tamarin moms. To foster the development of strong maternal bonds and attachment, let tamarin mothers tend to, groom, and bond with their offspring without undue interference.

Hand-rearing: To guarantee the survival and welfare of tamarin infants, hand-rearing protocols should be put into place in situations where mothers have been abandoned, neglected, or are unable to care for their offspring. Assist hand-reared infants with 24-hour care, feeding, and stimulation; adhere to recommended practices for preparing tamarin infant formula, feeding schedules, and developmental milestones.

Socialization and Integration: As soon as they are developmentally ready, assist hand-reared tamarin infants in socializing and integrating with their social group and conspecifics. Hand-reared infants should be gradually introduced to compatible group members, offering chances for supervised interactions, social learning, and bonding to support the infants' successful integration into the group.

VI. Conservation Implications and Ethical Issues

Ethical Breeding Practices: In captive tamarin breeding programs, uphold ethical breeding practices and animal welfare standards, giving the health, welfare, and natural behaviors of breeding individuals and their progeny first priority. Put policies in place to stop overbreeding, lessen stress, and lower the likelihood that breeding populations will experience reproductive health problems.

Conservation Education: Make use of captive tamarin breeding initiatives to raise public awareness of the value of primate conservation and the preservation of their habitats. By emphasizing the role of captive breeding in species conservation efforts through interpretive signage, educational programs, and outreach initiatives, you can engage visitors, students, and stakeholders.

Species Survival Plans: To support ex situ conservation efforts and genetic management initiatives, take part in cooperative breeding programs and regional and international species survival plans (SSPs) for endangered tamarin species. Work together with governmental organizations, zoological parks, and conservation groups to put SSP recommendations and conservation plans for at-risk tamarin species into practice.

Protecting the natural habitats of tamarin species and addressing threats like deforestation, habitat fragmentation, and the illegal wildlife trade are the goals of field research projects and habitat conservation initiatives. Encourage the preservation of community-based conservation projects and sustainable land management techniques in order to protect the tropical forests and biodiversity hotspots that are home to tamarins.

Tamarin breeding and reproduction are complex processes that call for careful consideration of behavioral, biological, and ethical aspects in order to protect the wellbeing and conservation of captive populations. Caregivers can support responsible ownership, conservation awareness, and the sustainability and genetic diversity of captive populations by learning about the reproductive biology, lifecycle patterns, and breeding management techniques of tamarin species. We are able to contribute to the long-term survival and welfare of these endearing and threatened primates both in captivity and in the wild by taking a comprehensive approach to tamarin reproduction and breeding.

Chapter 9

Regulations and Legal Aspects

In order to ensure the welfare, protection, and sustainable management of tamarins, legal considerations and regulations are essential to their ownership, trade, and conservation. The ownership and trade of tamarinds is regulated by a complex web of laws, permits, and regulations that are intended to protect their welfare, stop illegal trafficking, and advance conservation efforts. Tammars are highly regulated species that are subject to international, national, and regional legislation. We'll go over the laws and rules pertaining to tamarin ownership in this extensive guide, giving caregivers and other interested parties information on compliance requirements, permit processes, and conservation implications.

I. Status of International Conservation

The Convention on International Trade in Endangered Species of Wild Fauna and Flora (CITES) is a global agreement that regulates the international trade in threatened and endangered species. Tamarins are included in this list. Tamarin species are included in CITES Appendix II, which lists species that need regulation to ensure their survival and sustainable use but aren't necessarily in danger of going extinct.

Endangered Status: International conservation organizations like the International Union for Conservation of Nature (IUCN) have classified numerous tamarin species as either threatened or endangered. Their natural habitats are becoming fragmented, illegal wildlife trade, habitat loss, and deforestation are some of the factors that have led to their status as endangered.

Trade Restrictions: Live animals, specimens, and products derived from tamarins are subject to permits for import, export, and re-export under the terms of CITES, which places trade restrictions on tamarin species listed in Appendix II. The goals of these trade restrictions are to safeguard tamarin populations in the wild from overexploitation, control the commercial trade, and support conservation initiatives.

II. Regional and National Law

Wildlife Protection Laws: In an effort to preserve their native wildlife, including tamarins, numerous nations have passed laws and regulations pertaining to wildlife protection. The capture, ownership, sale, and transportation of tamarinds without the necessary licenses or permits may be restricted or outlawed by these laws.

Endangered Species Acts: Several nations have passed laws, known as Endangered Species Acts, with the express goal of preserving and protecting threatened and endangered species, such as tamarins. These laws may create fines for breaking wildlife protection regulations and offer legal safeguards for tamarind populations and their habitats.

Permit Requirements: National or regional wildlife authorities may impose permit requirements and regulatory oversight on tamarind ownership and trade. To ensure compliance with legal and conservation requirements, permits may be needed for activities like captive breeding, commercial trade, scientific research, and public exhibition of tamarins.

III. Licensing and Adherence to Regulations

Process of Getting Permits: In order to lawfully own, breed, trade, or display tamarin species, owners and caregivers may need to apply for and receive permits or licenses from the appropriate wildlife authorities. Usually, the permitting process entails meeting eligibility requirements, filing applications, paying fees, and providing supporting documentation.

Species Identification: To guarantee adherence to legal and conservation requirements, permit applications for tamarin ownership or trade may need precise species identification and supporting documentation. Give comprehensive details, including scientific names, provenance records, and origin and origin details, about the species, subspecies, or populations of tamarins that are involved.

Facility Standards: To protect the welfare and safety of captive tamarins, permitting authorities may set facility standards and guidelines for the housing, upkeep, and administration of these animals. Tamarind housing facilities could be the focus of evaluations, compliance audits, and inspections to make sure rules and regulations are being followed.

Requirements for Record-keeping: Tamarin owners and breeders might be expected to keep thorough records and paperwork about the purchase, transfer, breeding, and sale of tamarins. Maintain thorough records of all tamarin births, deaths, purchases, and transfers in addition to licenses, permits, and compliance paperwork.

IV. Moral Issues and Welfare Requirements

Animal Welfare Laws: In order to safeguard the welfare and general well-being of all animals, including tamarins, numerous nations have passed animal welfare laws and regulations. These laws may set requirements for veterinary care and enrichment, as well as for the housing, handling, and transportation of tamarinds.

Ethical Ownership Practices: It is recommended that tamarin owners and caregivers follow ethical ownership practices that put the health, welfare, and natural behaviors of tamarins first. In order to meet the physical, psychological, and social needs of tamarins while they are in captivity, provide suitable housing, food, socialization, and enrichment.

Breeders of Tamarins should adhere to responsible breeding practices that put the welfare of captive populations, health, and genetic diversity first. To aid in conservation efforts, refrain from overbreeding, inbreeding, or breeding people who have genetic disorders or inherited conditions. Instead, take part in cooperative breeding programs.

To increase public and breeder awareness of the importance, threats, and conservation status of tamarin species, it is recommended to promote conservation education and awareness among tamarin owners. To save tamarin populations and their habitats, support community-based conservation efforts, sustainable land use policies, and habitat conservation.

V. Consequences and Accountabilities for Conservation

Captive Breeding Programs: Take part in conservation efforts and captive breeding programs to support the genetic diversity and long-term viability of captive tamarin populations. Implement breeding guidelines, genetic management plans, and reintroduction initiatives for endangered tamarin species in cooperation with zoological parks, conservation groups, and governmental organizations.

Sustainable Trade Practices: To guarantee that individuals are lawfully obtained, ethically sourced, and not involved in the illegal wildlife trade, implement sustainable trade practices and ethical sourcing of tamarin species. Avoid buying or trading in animals that were illegally obtained or taken from the wild. Instead, acquire tamarins from respectable breeders, dealers, or organizations that have the necessary permits and paperwork.

Support initiatives and campaigns for habitat conservation that work to save the tamarin species' natural habitats and counteract threats like habitat loss, fragmentation, and deforestation. Encourage the preservation of conservation policies and sustainable land management techniques in order to protect tropical forests, biodiversity hotspots, and important habitat areas that are home to tamarins.

Involve local communities, stakeholders, and indigenous peoples in sustainable development initiatives and conservation campaigns that protect tamarin populations and their habitats. Work together with local partners to carry out habitat restoration projects, alternative livelihood programs, and community-based conservation initiatives that promote tamarin conservation and sustainable livelihoods.

VI. Monitoring and Enforcing Compliance

Regulatory Oversight: The laws, permits, and regulations pertaining to the ownership and trade of tamarinds that protect wildlife are subject to constant monitoring and enforcement by regulatory authorities, wildlife agencies, and enforcement agencies. Make sure tamarin owners and breeders are following the law and welfare regulations by conducting audits, compliance checks, and inspections.

Penalties and Enforcement Actions: There may be fines, penalties, or legal repercussions for breaking permit requirements, wildlife protection laws, or regulations pertaining to the ownership or trade of tamarinds. Revocation of permits, prosecution of offenders for wildlife trafficking or illegal possession of protected species, and confiscation of illegally held tamarins are examples of enforcement actions.

Public Reporting and Whistleblower Protection: Utilize whistleblower hotlines, reporting mechanisms, or online platforms to incentivize the public to report crimes pertaining to wildlife, the illegal wildlife trade, or violations of laws pertaining to tamarin welfare and conservation. Offer protection to witnesses and whistleblowers who disclose crimes involving wildlife or supply information that triggers legal action against those who traffic in or violate wildlife.

In order to maintain compliance with legal, ethical, and welfare standards for captive tamarin populations, legal considerations and regulations are essential to tamarin ownership, trade, and conservation. Caregivers can support the sustainability, welfare, and conservation of tamarin species in the wild and in captivity by being aware of and abiding by the international, national, and local laws that regulate tamarin ownership and trade. We can cooperate to save these endearing and endangered primates for future generations through ethical breeding programs, responsible ownership practices, and conservation awareness campaigns.

Chapter 10

Questions and Answers (FAQs) regarding Tamarin Pets

Exotic animal lovers are becoming more and more interested in keeping tamarinds as pets because they are fascinating and endearing primates. But having a tamarin has its own set of issues and difficulties, which raises a number of queries from both potential and existing owners. We'll cover common questions (FAQs) regarding tamarin pets in this extensive guide, offering thorough explanations and valuable insights to assist both current and potential owners in making the best decisions for their primates.

I. Common Queries Regarding Tamarins

- Tamarins: what are they?

Tamarins are small to medium-sized New World monkeys that are members of the Leontopithecus or Saguinus genus. They are renowned for their unusual appearance, social behavior, and vocalizations. They are native to the tropical forests of Central and South America.

- Which tamarin species are most frequently kept as pets?

The cotton-top tamarin (Saguinus oedipus), the emperor tamarin (Saguinus imperator), the golden lion tamarin (Leontopithecus rosalia), and the pygmy marmoset (Cebuella pygmaea) are common species of tamarins kept as pets.

- Is it permissible to own tamarins as pets?

The legality of keeping tamarins as pets varies according to regional, governmental, and global laws. Tamarins are categorized as exotic animals in many jurisdictions, meaning that owning one may need permits, licenses, or other special permissions.

- What qualities make tamarins suitable pets? Tamarins are intelligent, gregarious, active primates with intricate care needs. To thrive in captivity, they need roomy enclosures, a varied diet, social interaction, and mental stimulation.

II. Tamarin Care and Husbandry

What kind of enclosure is necessary for tamarins? Tamarins need large, safe enclosures with lots of vertical room for exploration and climbing. To encourage natural behaviors, enclosures should be furnished with branches, perches, ropes, and enrichment materials.

- What nourish tamarinds?

Due to their omnivorous nature, tamarinds need a diverse diet that includes fruits, vegetables, insects, and lean meats or eggs as a source of protein. Tamarins can receive a balanced diet from commercial primates, supplemented with fresh produce and occasional treats.

- How are tamarins socialized?

Tamarins are gregarious creatures that enjoy company and interaction. Tamarins can be socialized by enrichment activities, supervised play sessions with humans and conspecifics, and positive reinforcement training.

- Do tamarinds need to be taken to the vet?

In order to preserve their health and wellbeing, tamarinds need to have routine veterinary examinations, shots, and preventive care. To give tamarins specialized care, look for a veterinarian who specializes in exotic animal medicine.

III. Tamarind Behavior and Training

- Are tamarins trainable?

Indeed, tamarins can be trained to learn a range of behaviors, such as recall, targeting, and stationing, by employing positive reinforcement techniques. For tamarins kept in captivity, training can improve mental stimulation, cooperation, and communication.

- How can behavioral problems in tamarins be resolved?

Tamarind behavioral problems can be resolved by using positive reinforcement training, environmental enrichment, and treating underlying causes like boredom, stress, or social isolation. For help with behavior modification, speak with a licensed veterinarian or animal behaviorist.

- Do tamarins and their owners form a bond?

Tamarins and their human caretakers can develop close relationships via consistent communication, reinforcement, and mutual trust. Establishing a rapport and trust with tamarins requires consistency in handling and care, as well as time and patience.

- Are tamarins hostile animals?

Although it is uncommon, situations such as territorial disputes, mating competition, or fear-based aggression can lead to tamarind aggression. Anger can be avoided and dealt with by being aware of tamarin body language, social dynamics, and stress triggers.

IV. Legal and Ethical Aspects of Owning a Tamarin

- Is it permissible to keep tamarins as pets?

Legal considerations and regulations, such as licenses, permits, and wildlife protection laws, apply to the ownership of tabarin. Before obtaining a pet tamarin, familiarize yourself with local, national, and international regulations regarding tamarin ownership.

- What moral implications come with being a tamarin owner?

Tamarin ownership involves ethical considerations such as giving them proper care, attending to their physical and psychological needs, honoring their natural behaviors, and supporting initiatives aimed at preserving wild tamarin populations.

- How can I make sure that the legal conditions for owning a tamarin are met?

Assure adherence to facility standards and welfare guidelines, obtain required permits or licenses, and stay up to date on any changes to wildlife protection laws and regulations in order to ensure compliance with legal requirements for tamarin ownership.

- What effects does owning a tamarin have on conservation?

Keeping a tamarin as a pet can have positive effects on conservation. These effects can include promoting captive breeding initiatives, increasing public awareness of tamarin conservation issues, and aiding in the advocacy and education efforts to preserve habitat.

V. Tamarins' Health and Veterinary Care

Which health conditions are common in tamarins?
Tamarins frequently experience respiratory infections, gastrointestinal disorders, dental issues, and parasitic infections. Preventive care and routine veterinary exams can help spot and treat health problems early.

- How can one locate a veterinarian for a tamarin pet?

To provide your pet tamarins with specialized care, look for a veterinarian who specializes in primatology and exotic animal medicine. Seek advice from nearby zoos, wildlife rehabilitation facilities, or exotic animal rescue groups regarding veterinarians who specialize in tamarin care.

- Which vaccines are required for tamarinds?

Tamarins may need to be vaccinated against common infectious diseases like tetanus, hepatitis, and rabies, depending on the prevalence of the disease in their area and the risk of exposure. To create a vaccination schedule specific to your pet tamarin's requirements, speak with a veterinarian.

- How do you give your pet tamarins enrichment?

Using a range of environmental, social, and cognitive stimulation activities—such as climbing frames, foraging puzzles, sensory experiences, and interactive play—you can provide your pet tamarins with enrichment. To keep interest levels high and avoid habituation, rotate enrichment materials frequently.

Tamarins have special needs, behaviors, and legal requirements that must be carefully considered before owning one as a pet. It can be a rewarding but difficult experience. Caregivers can make well-informed decisions, give the best care possible, and advance the welfare and conservation of these endearing primates by answering commonly asked questions regarding tamarin ownership. Pet owners can have a rewarding and enriching relationship with their primates while also supporting global conservation efforts for tamarin species if they provide the right care, comprehend, and respect for tamarins' natural behaviors and habitats."

www.ingramcontent.com/pod-product-compliance
Lightning Source LLC
Chambersburg PA
CBHW051822250726

48659CB00005B/1628